MW00568766

Five Bears All in a Den

By Susi Jones

Illustrated by
Daniel J. Mahoney

Target Skill Character

PEARSON

Scott
Foresman

Five bears are all in a den—
Mom, Dad, and three cubs.

Mom lifts one paw.

Dad lifts two paws.

All three cubs lift their paws.

Mom walks to the river.

Dad walks to the river.

Three cubs run to the river.

Mom traps one fish.

Dad traps two fish.

Three cubs trap three,
four, five fish.

Mom naps. Dad naps.

Three cubs climb the tree.

Mom calls. Dad calls.

Three cubs run.

Run, run, run!

Five bears are all in a den—
Mom, Dad, and three cubs.